RETIRED?!

Quips and Quotes for When Every Day is Saturday

summersdale

RETIRED?!

An Hachette UK Company
www.hachette.co.uk

Summersdale Publishers Ltd
Part of Octopus Publishing Group Limited
Carmelite House
50 Victoria Embankment
LONDON
EC4Y 0DZ
UK

www.summersdale.com

Printed and bound in Croatia

ISBN: 978-1-78685-530-5

Substantial discounts on bulk quantities of Summersdale books are available to corporations, professional associations and other organisations. For details contact general enquiries: telephone: +44 (0) 1243 771107 or email: enquiries@summersdale.com.

To.............................

From...........................

After 30, a body has a mind of its own.

BETTE MIDLER

'Gosh,' thought Harry, 'you really get to know your partner once you're both retired.'

Retirement is wonderful. It's doing nothing without worrying about getting caught at it.

GENE PERRET

LIFE HAS GOT TO BE LIVED. THAT'S ALL THERE IS TO IT.

Eleanor Roosevelt

There's never enough time to do all the nothing you want.

BILL WATTERSON

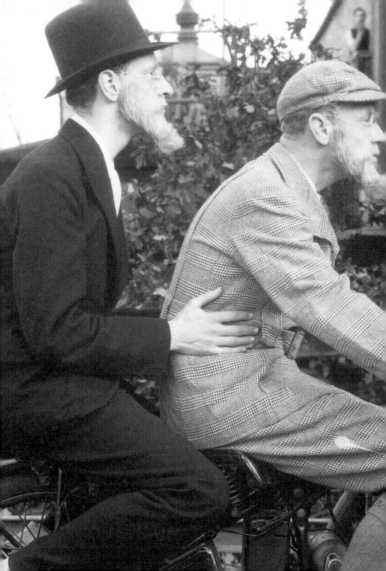

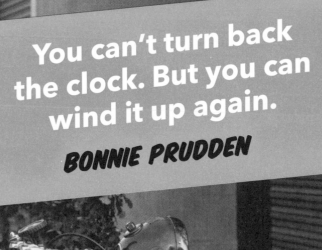

You can't turn back the clock. But you can wind it up again.

BONNIE PRUDDEN

How pleasant is the day when we give up striving to be young or slender.

WILLIAM JAMES

'Retired, but with my finger still on the pulse,' Ron thought to himself.

I would rather be round and jolly than thin and cross.

ANN WIDDECOMBE

**Between two evils,
I always pick the one I
never tried before.**

MAE WEST

*I THINK YOUR WHOLE
LIFE SHOWS IN YOUR FACE,
AND YOU SHOULD BE
PROUD OF THAT.*

Lauren Bacall

A comfortable old age is the reward of a well-spent youth.

MAURICE CHEVALIER

The trouble with retirement is that you never get a day off.

ABE LEMONS

Goodbye tension, hello pension!

We learn from experience
that men never learn
anything from experience.

GEORGE BERNARD SHAW

I MEAN, WHAT'S SO
FULFILLING ABOUT
FULFILMENT ANYWAY?

Maureen Lipman

I've never met
a woman in my life
who would give up
lunch for sex.

ERMA BOMBECK

When a man retires, his wife gets twice the husband but only half the income.

CHI-CHI RODRIGUEZ

It is time I stepped aside for a less experienced and less able man.

SCOTT ELLEDGE

When you're retired, you can get a Saturday job pulling pints behind the bar, just like you always wanted.

Men don't get cellulite. God might just be a man.

RITA RUDNER

There's one advantage to being 102. There's no peer pressure.

DENNIS WOLFBERG

I'M NOT SIXTY, I'M 'SEXTY'.

Dolly Parton

Man's life is a progress, not a station.

RALPH WALDO EMERSON

Retire from work,
but not from life.

M. K. SONI

Welcome to your annual 52-week holiday!

I keep fit. Every morning, I do a hundred laps of an Olympic-sized swimming pool – in a small motor launch.

PETER COOK

WHEN PEOPLE TELL YOU HOW YOUNG YOU LOOK, THEY ARE TELLING YOU HOW OLD YOU ARE.

Cary Grant

Nobody can go back and start a new beginning, but anyone can start today and make a new ending.

MARIA ROBINSON

You are only young once, but you can stay immature indefinitely.

OGDEN NASH

When I'm old and grey,
I want to have a house
by the sea... And a damn
good kitchen to cook in.

AVA GARDNER

Ike and Nora were really starting to notice the impact of health-and-safety culture on their usual exercise class.

Old gardeners don't die. They just throw in the trowel.

ANONYMOUS

For us elderly people, not owning a computer is like not having a headache.

EDWARD ENFIELD

THE MORE SIDE ROADS YOU STOP TO EXPLORE, THE LESS LIKELY THAT LIFE WILL PASS YOU BY.

Robert Brault

I don't want to retire.
I'm not that good at
crossword puzzles.

NORMAN MAILER

You know you're getting on a bit when you can't go to church without the priest offering you the last rites.

Don't simply retire from something; have something to retire to.

HARRY EMERSON FOSDICK

Good wine is a necessity of life for me.

THOMAS JEFFERSON

ONE SHOULD NEVER MAKE ONE'S DEBUT WITH A SCANDAL. ONE SHOULD RESERVE THAT TO GIVE AN INTEREST TO ONE'S OLD AGE.

Oscar Wilde

When it comes
to staying young,
a mind-lift beats
a face-lift any day.

MARTY BUCELLA

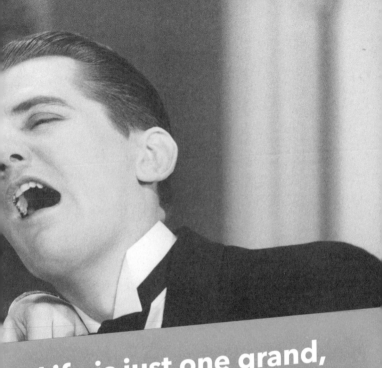

Life is just one grand, sweet song, so start the music.

RONALD REAGAN

What do gardeners do when they retire?

BOB MONKHOUSE

'Just think,' her son said, 'you'll be able to babysit all the time!'

The past is a guidepost, not a hitching post.

L. THOMAS HOLDCROFT

**The older I get,
the better I used to be.**

LEE TREVINO

IF YOU ENJOY LIVING, IT IS
NOT DIFFICULT TO KEEP THE
SENSE OF WONDER.

Ray Bradbury

Live each day as if it were your last, and garden as though you will live forever.

ANONYMOUS

An old man looks permanent, as if he had been born an old man.

H. E. BATES

'Thank heavens I was born before clean eating and fad diets!'

One ought, every day at least, to hear a little song, read a good poem, see a fine picture, and, if it were possible, to speak a few reasonable words.

JOHANN WOLFGANG VON GOETHE

THE AGEING PROCESS HAS YOU FIRMLY IN ITS GRASP IF YOU NEVER GET THE URGE TO THROW A SNOWBALL.

Doug Larson

Just the simple act of tasting a glass of wine is its own event.

DAVID HYDE PIERCE

One Martini is all right.
Two are too many, and
three are not enough.

JAMES THURBER

Sometimes Geoff rather thought he preferred life with glasses off.

I don't answer the phone. I get the feeling whenever I do that there will be someone on the other end.

FRED COUPLES

Getting old is a fascinating thing. The older you get, the older you want to get!

KEITH RICHARDS

My wife said to me, 'I don't look fifty, do I darling?' I said, 'Not any more.'

BOB MONKHOUSE

IN OLD AGE WE ARE LIKE A BATCH OF LETTERS THAT SOMEONE HAS SENT. WE ARE NO LONGER IN THE PAST, WE HAVE ARRIVED.

Knut Hamsun

When you reach retirement, you switch bosses – from the one who hired you to the one who married you.

GENE PERRET

I'm 42 around the chest, 52 around the waist, 92 around the golf course and a nuisance around the house.

GROUCHO MARX

Retirement:
when your outdoor
clothes become your
indoor clothes.

The key to a happy retirement is to have enough money to live on, but not enough to worry about.

ANONYMOUS

ANYONE WHO KEEPS THE ABILITY TO SEE BEAUTY NEVER GROWS OLD.

Franz Kafka

Fun is like
life insurance; the
older you get, the
more it costs.

KIN HUBBARD

'Let's face it, Stan –
we can no longer
get away with the
current fashions.'

Ethel had the sudden realisation that now she had retired, every hour was happy hour.

In your retirement years, never drink coffee at lunch; it will keep you awake in the afternoon.

ANONYMOUS

Eventually you will reach a point when you stop lying about your age and start bragging about it.

WILL ROGERS

If I am doing nothing, I like to be doing nothing to some purpose. That is what leisure means.

ALAN BENNETT

LAUGHTER DOESN'T REQUIRE TEETH.

Bill Newton

No man is ever old enough to know better.

HOLBROOK JACKSON

A little nonsense now and then is relished by the wisest men.

ANONYMOUS

Eventually, Harold had to break it to his wife that the supermarket had sold out of Prosecco.

Wisdom doesn't necessarily come with age. Sometimes age just shows up all by itself.

TOM WILSON

WHEN MEN REACH THEIR SIXTIES AND RETIRE, THEY GO TO PIECES. WOMEN GO RIGHT ON COOKING.

Gail Sheehy

No man loves life like
him that's growing old.

SOPHOCLES

Gardens are not made by singing 'Oh, how beautiful', and sitting in the shade.

RUDYARD KIPLING

Mildred was on an amazing new diet where you ate everything and prayed for a miracle.

Old age is an excellent time for outrage. My goal is to say or do at least one outrageous thing every week.

MAGGIE KUHN

I still find each day too short for all the thoughts I want to think, all the walks I want to take… and all the friends I want to see.

JOHN BURROUGHS

Older people shouldn't eat health food – they need all the preservatives they can get.

ROBERT ORBEN

I STILL HAVE A FULL DECK; I JUST SHUFFLE SLOWER NOW.

Anonymous

There is no pleasure
worth forgoing just for
an extra three years in
the geriatric ward.

JOHN MORTIMER

We're fools whether
we dance or not, so we
might as well dance.

JAPANESE PROVERB

The only downside to having a hubby so hot you want to tear his cardigan off, is that you're usually the one sewing the buttons on again.

Don't worry about avoiding temptation. As you grow older, it starts avoiding you.

ANONYMOUS

AGE IS ONLY A NUMBER.

Lexi Starling

The best time to
start thinking about
your retirement is
before the boss does.

ANONYMOUS

There's one thing I always wanted to do before I quit: retire!

GROUCHO MARX

You know you're getting old when you're dashing through Marks and Spencer, spot a pair of Dr Scholl's sandals, stop, and think, 'Hmm, they look comfy.'

VICTORIA WOOD

There is life
after retirement,
and it is better.

CATHERINE PULSIFER

If you're interested in finding out more about our books, find us on Facebook at **Summersdale Publishers** and follow us on Twitter at **@Summersdale**.

www.summersdale.com

IMAGE CREDITS